Originally published in France in 1995 under the title *Atlas du ciel* by Gallimard Jeunesse.

Copyright © 2005 by Editions Gallimard Jeunesse.

This edition English translation by J. Elizabeth Mills copyright © 2005 by Scholastic Inc.

SCHOLASTIC, SCHOLASTIC REFERENCE, and associated logos are trademarks and/or registered trademarks of Scholastic Inc. All other trademarks used in this book are owned by their respective trademark owners.

No part of this publication may be reproduced, stored in a retrieval system, or transmitted in any form or by any means, electronic, mechanical, photocopying, recording, or otherwise, without written permission of the publisher. For information regarding permission, write to Scholastic Inc., Attention: Permissions Department, 557 Broadway, New York, NY 10012.

ISBN-13: 978-0-545-00146-5
ISBN-10: 0-545-00146-3

12 11 10 9 8 7 6 5 4 3 2 1

Printed in Italy.

SCHOLASTIC FIRST DISCOVERY

The Universe

Created by Gallimard Jeunesse
and Jean-Pierre Verdet
Illustrated by Donald Grant

SCHOLASTIC REFERENCE
an imprint of
SCHOLASTIC

Many astronomers believe the universe was born from one gigantic explosion called the big bang.

**Turn the pages
to discover
our universe!**

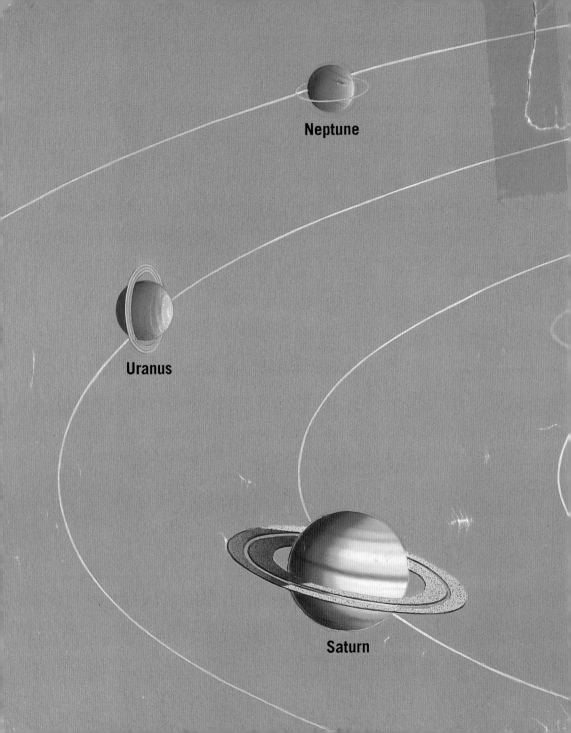

Neptune

Uranus

Saturn

Eight planets orbit around the sun.
They make up the solar system.

Jupiter

Mars

Venus

Sun

Earth

Mercury

It takes Earth one year to spin, or orbit, around the sun.

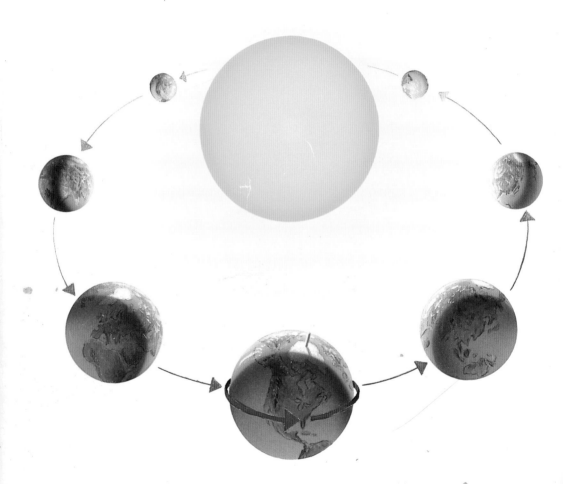

It takes Earth 24 hours, or one day, to revolve around itself once.

The moon orbits Earth
in one month, approximately.

From 1969 to 1972, we sent astronauts to
an enormous, rocky sphere called the moon.

The moon's surface is covered with craters.

The astronauts walked on the moon and rode in vehicles. They brought back many rock samples.

Earth is made up of an atmosphere, a crust, a mantle, an outer core, and an inner core.

**Planets do not glow with their own light—
they reflect the light of the sun.**

Mars, Mercury, and Venus
are solid planets like Earth.

Mars is easily
recognized by its
red surface and
its polar ice caps.

Mercury, a giant
rock, is very
close to the sun.

Under the heavy atmosphere on Venus,
there is an uneven surface marked by
valleys, mountains, and volcanoes.

Now discover these planets!

Jupiter is the biggest.
It is made up of many gases.

The space probe
Voyager
visited Venus.

Saturn has
beautiful rings.

Uranus and Neptune are
also gaseous planets.

The sun shines with its own light
because it is made up of
extremely hot gases.

Satellites have come
close to the sun
and transmitted their
observations by radio waves.

The sun's surface is grainy,
like an orange peel,
and has a temperature of nearly
10,000 degrees Fahrenheit!

**Dark spots sometimes appear on the sun—
they are cool areas. Gigantic arcs of
burning gas surround the sun.**

With the naked eye, several thousand stars can be seen. With binoculars, hundreds of thousands of stars can be seen. With a telescope, millions can be seen!

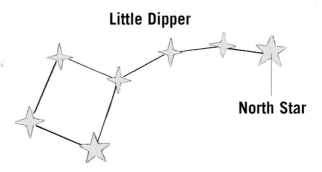

Little Dipper

North Star

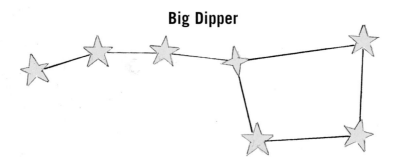

Big Dipper

All stars seem to turn around one star— the North Star.

At the end of their life,
stars diminish, sometimes explode...

...and then become so tiny
they are called dwarf stars.

Our galaxy is called the Milky Way.
Here is the Milky Way from above.
It is a large, flat spiral, filled with billions of stars.

Four large arms
spin out of its core

Here is a view of our
galaxy from the side

In the sky, there are
millions and millions
of other galaxies
of different shapes.

Some memorable moments in space history...

Laika, a dog, was the first living being to enter orbit (November 3, 1957).

The Russian satellite *Sputnik* was the first artificial satellite (October 4, 1957).

The Russian Yuri Gagarin was the first man in space (April 12, 1961).

Neil Armstrong, Edwin "Buzz" Aldrin, and Michael Collins were the first men to travel to the moon (July 21, 1969).

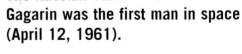

The space station *Salyut 1* was launched in 1971 by the USSR.

The American space telescope *Hubble* was put into orbit (April 25, 1990).

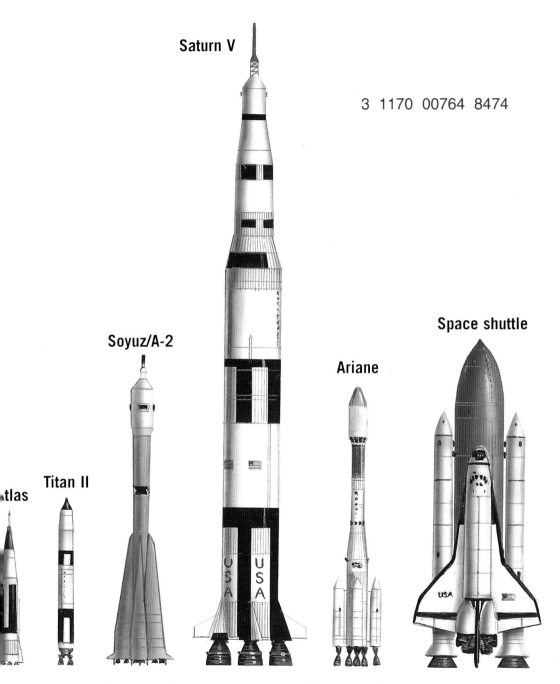

Saturn V

Space shuttle

Soyuz/A-2

Ariane

tlas

Titan II

...and some powerful engines.